Utterly Gorgeous FASHION

NATALIE ABADZIS

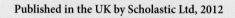

Scholastic Children's Books,
Euston House, 24 Eversholt Street,
London NW1 1DB, UK

A division of Scholastic Ltd
London ~ New York ~ Toronto ~ Sydney ~ Auckland
Mexico City ~ New Delhi ~ Hong Kong

Published in the UK by Scholastic Ltd, 2012

Text and artwork © Scholastic Ltd, 2012

Text by Natalie Abadzis
Illustrations by Natalie Abadzis
Crafts by Natalie Abadzis
Art Editor: Katie Knutton
Photography by Simon Anning and Barry Hayden
Edited by Sally Morgan

ISBN 978 1407 120928

Printed and bound by Tien Wah Press Pte. Ltd, Singapore

2 4 6 8 10 9 7 5 3 1

Papers used by Scholastic Children's Books are made from woods grown in sustainable forests.

Utterly Gorgeous Contents

Things you will need

Here's all you need to make a cool collection of Utterly Gorgeous Fashion crafts!

gloves

white paper

paintbrushes

fabric paint

scissors

dress

pins

fabric glue

long-sleeved top

rubber gloves

toothbrush

pom poms

pinking shears

Velcro dots

iron

wired feathers

selection of foam

newspaper

drinking straw

rubber bands

legging

selection of felt

iron-on fabric adhesive

tracing paper

hair band

sunglasses

sequins

pumps

cocktail stick

chain

red glitter

sequin trim

salt

masking tape

hair bands

paper fasteners

ruler

ricrack

hooded top

pencils

double-sided tape

thin black pen

permanent marker

thick black pen

jeans

shorts

canvas tote

plastic bag

jacket

plimsolls

bottle lid

beret

scarf

sponge

plastic sleeve

needle and thread

gems

acrylic paint

fabric paint pen

beads

fabric scraps

plate

cold-water dye

ribbon

skirt

jumper

bucket

vest tops

pegs

T-shirts

stick

clear nail varnish

5

City chic!

Get Parisian pretty with this Arc de Triumph of a vest!

1 Trace and cut out the templates on page 63.

2 Cut a section out of an old T-shirt. Place your T-shirt material underneath a piece of iron-on fabric adhesive, and ask an adult to iron it into place.

3 Draw around your templates onto the adhesive side of your T-shirt material, and cut them out.

Handy tip!

If you don't have any iron-on fabric adhesive, why not try using fabric glue? Experiment with any shapes you like.

4 Arrange your shapes, fabric side up, onto your vest. Ask an adult to fix them into position using an iron.

Bow beautiful

Get your style all tied up with these on-trend bows.

1 Cut two rectangles out of a piece of bright felt – one measuring 15 x 18 cm and another 6 x 3 cm.

2 Pinch the larger piece of felt in the middle and wrap the smaller piece around the pinch, to gather it together. Glue the ends of the smaller piece at the back using fabric glue.

3 Stick on some sequins using fabric glue and leave it to dry. Glue your bow onto any item of clothing, or accessory you like.

Why not tie a bow around the strap of a plain vest? Beautiful!

Lovely leggings

Hit the refresh button and give your leggings a cherry-twist makeover!

You will need

1 Line the inside your leggings with newspaper. Dip the top of a bottle lid into some fabric paint and press it onto your leggings. Repeat this all over the front of your leggings and leave to dry.

2 Use a paintbrush and some green fabric paint to add a stalk and some leaves and leave to dry. Repeat your design on the other side, before leaving to dry again. Ask an adult to set your design using an iron, following the instructions on the fabric paint.

Super-sweet shrug

You will need

Turn any old sweatshirt or hoodie into a super-stylish shrug!

1 Use your scissors to cut 10 cm off each arm of your sweatshirt and then roll up the sleeves a little.

Handy tip!

Change the colour of ribbon to suit your mood!

2 If your sweatshirt has a hood, cut it off and then trim away the bottom half of your sweatshirt.

3 Draw a line down the centre of the top. Draw curved lines starting from the top of the centre line, curving out to the bottom left and right corner of your top. Cut along the curved lines, being careful to avoid snipping the back.

4 Use scissors to make two holes 2 cm away from the collar. Thread a piece of ribbon through one hole and tie a knot behind the hole. Repeat on the other side. Tie the two ribbons in a bow.

Glam gloves

Wave goodbye to dull winter gloves wearing these utterly gorgeous mittens!

You will need

Add some studs for a wild rock look!

Metal mitts

Take a pair of black gloves, fingerless are best, and use a needle and thread to sew on some broken necklace chains.

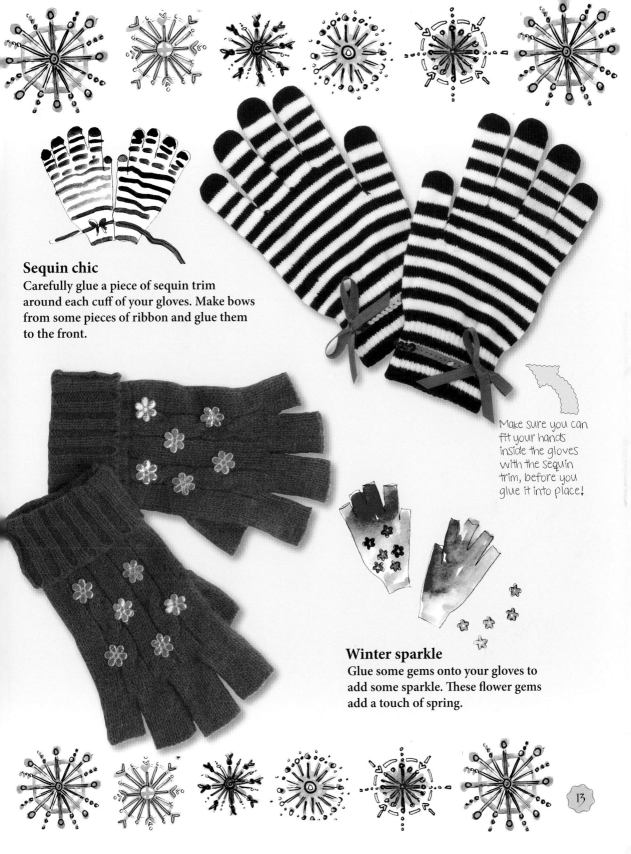

Sequin chic

Carefully glue a piece of sequin trim around each cuff of your gloves. Make bows from some pieces of ribbon and glue them to the front.

Make sure you can fit your hands inside the gloves with the sequin trim, before you glue it into place!

Winter sparkle

Glue some gems onto your gloves to add some sparkle. These flower gems add a touch of spring.

13

Cherry blossom

Look petal perfect with this beautiful blossom Tee!

1 Place newspaper inside your T-shirt.

2 Use a paintbrush to make long strokes with watered-down fabric paint, down from the neck of your T-shirt.

3 Add some blobs of watered-down paint at the bottom and leave to dry.

4 Add blossom by making circles of five blobs of paint for petals and adding dots in another colour for the middle. Leave to dry. Ask an adult to fix your design using an iron, following the instructions on the fabric paint.

Add more blobs
of fabric paint to
create a shower
of falling petals!

Denim skirt

Recycle your old jeans into a fab new skirt for summer.

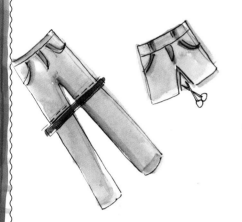

1 Cut the legs of your jeans to the length you would like your skirt. You now have a pair of shorts. Cut up the seams of the inside leg to the crotch.

2 To stop the triangular gap at the front and back of your skirt from fraying, fold the edges inwards and stick them down with fabric glue. Leave to dry.

3 Cut two triangle shapes, slightly bigger than the gaps in the front and back of your skirt, from the leftover legs of your jeans. Glue these to the inside of your skirt to fill in the gaps and leave to dry.

4 Trim away any excess from the bottom of your skirt. Don't worry if the bottom edges are frayed, this will add a distressed look. Glue some sticky gems to the front.

Why not attach an old bracelet to one of the belt loops?

Handy tip!
To make your skirt extra secure, fix the triangles in place using running stitch, see page 62.

Ruby slippers

Follow those glittery red pumps!
Follow, follow, follow…

You will need

1 Dip your sponge into some red acrylic paint, and use it to dab paint all over your pumps. Leave to dry.

2 Spread glue all over your pumps and sprinkle on the glitter. Leave to dry.

3 Cut a red pompom in half and glue a piece to the front of each pump. Now, click your heels together and fly over the rainbow!

Denim tote bag

Get carried away in style with a cheeky trouser-leg tote!

You will need

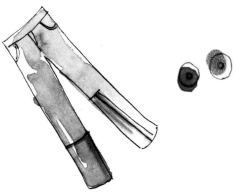

1 Use a pair of sharp scissors to cut a 22 cm section from the bottom of one leg of your jeans. Measure and cut two, 30 x 4 cm strips from the other leg, to make the handles.

2 Turn the bag section inside out. Fold 2 cm over at the top and stick down using fabric glue. Leave to dry. Turn the bag right side out and glue the handles to the inside top edge of your bag. Glue the bottom edges of the bag together. Leave to dry.

3 Use fabric glue to stick strips of sparkly sequin trim to the front of the bag for decoration.

4 Trace and cut out the bird template from page 64. Draw around it onto some felt and cut out your bird shape. Glue to the front of your bag with a gem for the eye.

Glue on more gems to add stars to your sky scene.

Party plimsolls

Get one step ahead of the game
in these perfect plimsolls!

Twinkle toes
Stick sequin stars to the toe and along
the sides of each plimsoll using fabric
glue. Replace the laces with brightly
contrasting ribbon.

Art attack
Use a toothbrush and your thumb to
flick fabric paint onto some white
plimsolls. Leave each layer of colour to
dry, before you splatter on another.

Cool waves

Cut pieces of coloured rickrack long enough to reach from the top to the toe of your plimsolls. Cut them at an angle so that the ends sit neatly against the seams of the shoes. Fix in place with fabric glue. Use a cocktail stick to glue on some gems. Leave to dry.

Try using some satin ribbon instead of rickrack for a more princessy vibe.

Funky fringed top

Snip, trim and style old into new with this stylish little top!

You will need

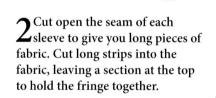

1 Cut the sleeves off your T-shirt with sharp scissors to turn it into a vest.

2 Cut open the seam of each sleeve to give you long pieces of fabric. Cut long strips into the fabric, leaving a section at the top to hold the fringe together.

3 Use fabric glue to stick these pieces to one shoulder of your shirt and leave to dry.

4 Snip slashes into the front layer of your T-shirt. Repeat on the back of the T-shirt if you wish.

Handy tip!
Wear your new top over a bright vest so it shows through the slashes.

Ahoy there, style!

Turn some old jeans into a cute, nautical belt!

Why not use iron—on fabric adhesive for your hems, instead of fabric glue. Find out how on page 62.

You will need

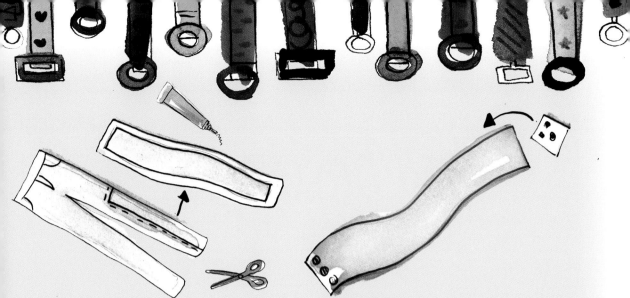

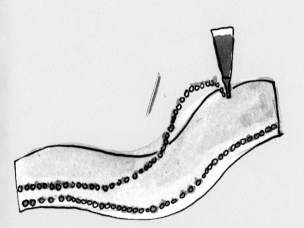

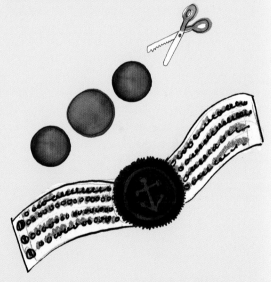

1 Cut a rectangle, measuring 80 x 10 cm, from the leg of your jeans. Apply fabric glue along each side of your rectangle, 1 cm in from the edge. Fold over each edge, into the glue, to make a hem.

2 Stick self-adhesive Velcro dots to each end of the belt so you can fasten it.

3 Use a cocktail stick to apply fabric glue to some strips of sequin trim and stick them to your belt. Leave to dry.

4 Trace and cut out the templates on page 64. Draw around them onto some bright felt and cut out the shapes. Glue the shapes together and attach to the front of the belt using fabric glue.

Beautiful berets

Hats off to these
gorgeous berets!

You will need

Snowy sparkler

1 Cut some strips of sequin trim.
Apply fabric glue to the back of the
sequin trim using a cocktail stick and
attach to the beret.

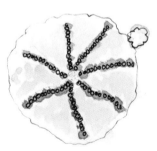

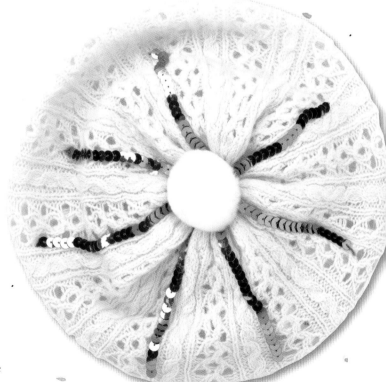

2 Glue a large pompom to the centre
of the beret. Leave to dry.

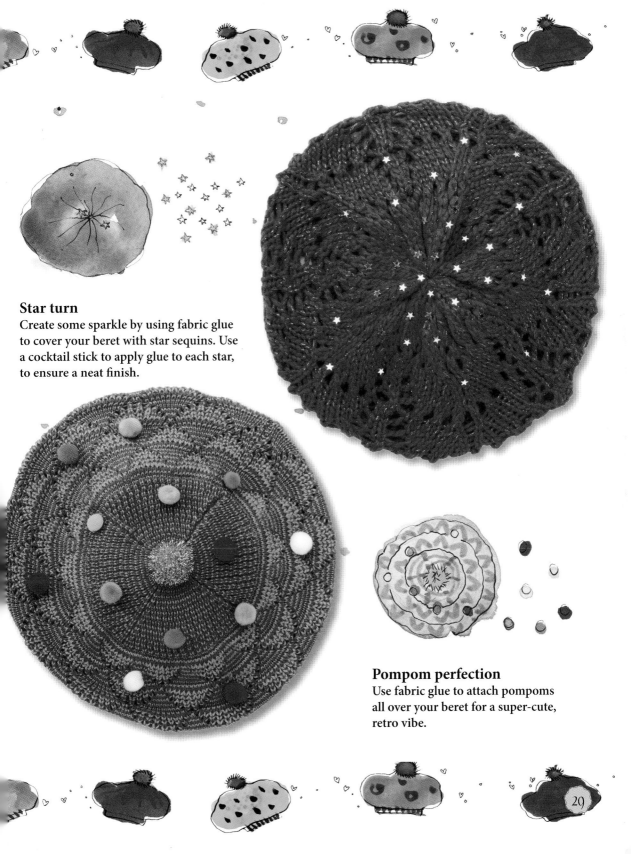

Star turn

Create some sparkle by using fabric glue to cover your beret with star sequins. Use a cocktail stick to apply glue to each star, to ensure a neat finish.

Pompom perfection

Use fabric glue to attach pompoms all over your beret for a super-cute, retro vibe.

Super spots

Get spotted in this daring dotty design.

You will need

1 Dip the end of the pencil into some fabric paint and use it dab paint onto your vest. Leave to dry. Ask an adult to fix your design using an iron.

2 Glue an old string of beads or pearls around the neck for a super-chic look.

Handy tip!

Use pencil-topper polka dots to brighten up all of your tired vests and Tees.

Striped shorts

You will need

Get your wardrobe ready for some summer sun with these retro disco shorts.

1 Stick strips of masking tape down the front of your shorts. Use a paintbrush to apply fabric paint between the strips of tape. Leave to dry.

2 Peel off the masking tape. Paint stripes of fabric paint, in another colour, next to the first. Leave to dry. Ask an adult to fix your design using an iron, following the instructions on the fabric paint.

Team with a sparkly belt for a show-stopping circus look.

Festival tie-dye

Give your wardrobe a festival vibe with some summery tie-dye to die for!

Bright bag

1 Take the centre of the bag and bunch it up. Wrap an elastic band around it. Keep adding bands at regular intervals.

2 Put on your rubber gloves and dunk your bag in the bucket of dye, salt and cold water, following the instructions on the packet.

3 Take your bag out, after the time indicated on the packet, remove the elastic bands and rinse thoroughly. Fix your dye design following the instructions on the packet. Leave to dry.

DRess to impress

1 Fold the dress as you would make a fan from a piece of paper. Use clothes pegs to hold your folds in place.

Use a stick to stir the dye from time to time.

2 Make up your dye with cold water and salt in a bucket, following the instructions on the packet. Wearing rubber gloves, put your dress into the bucket of dye.

3 Take your dress out after the time indicated on the packet, remove the pegs, and rinse thoroughly. Fix your dye design following the instructions and leave to dry.

Street art shirt

Go wild with this urban graffiti design!

You will need

1 Place a plastic bag inside your T-shirt. Use fabric paint and a thick paintbrush to make some abstract squiggles on your shirt. Leave to dry.

2 Add some more abstract squiggles in another colour. Leave to dry.

3 Add a third colour and leave to dry.

4 Lastly add your writing to your design using a thinner paintbrush and black fabric paint. Ask an adult to fix your design using an iron, following the instructions on the fabric paint.

Handy tip!

To get a scratchy graffiti effect, dip a thin brush in fabric paint and wipe off the excess before you begin writing.

Funky legwarmers

You will need

Rock the dance floor in these super-sassy winter warmers!

1 Use a pair of sharp scissors to cut the sleeves off your top.

2 Turn the sleeves inside out and fold down 1 cm at the top of each sleeve. Stick down with fabric glue. Leave to dry. Turn your sleeves right side out.

3 Take a piece of ribbon and stitch it to the top of one of your sleeves using running stitch (see page 62), leaving the ends open at one side. Repeat for the other sleeve.

4 To finish your lovely legwarmers, simply tie the ends of the ribbons into pretty bows!

Messy print jeans

Channel your inner rock chick in messy print denim.

1 Cut a chunky rectangle from the end of an old sponge.

2 Place some newspaper inside your jeans.

Handy tip!

Try printing with different shapes!

3 Dip your sponge into your fabric paint and use it to dab paint onto your jeans as messily and randomly as possible. Leave to dry.

Tie an old chain to the belt loop for a rocking, punk look!

4 Sponge on some more paint in a different colour. Leave to dry. Ask an adult to fix your design using an iron, following the instruction on the fabric paint.

Fruity cutie

Give an old pair of jeans a fresh
and fruity summer look!

You will need

1 Cut the legs off your jeans to transform them
into shorts. Cut the legs longer than your want
your shorts, so that you can turn them up.

2 Roll up the legs of your shorts to the length you
would like to wear them.

For a funkier look, cut
your shapes out using
pinking shears and
experiment with different
fabrics and ribbons.

3 Trace and cut out the template on page 64. Draw around the apple shape onto a bright piece of fabric. Cut out a square of contrasting fabric, larger than your apple.

4 Cut out your apple and then glue your shapes onto the back pocket of your shorts using fabric glue. Leave them to dry. Finish your shorts by adding an old silk scarf for a belt. Gorgeous!

Star stencils

Shoot some stars across your vest!

1 Place some newspaper inside your vest.

2 Place a clear plastic folder onto the star template on page 63. Trace the star shapes using a permanent marker. Pierce the centre of each star with your scissors and cut them out from the inside.

You will need

3 Position the stencil onto your vest. Dab fabric paint onto your stencil using a paintbrush, so that paint goes through the stars and onto the fabric. Leave to dry. Ask an adult to fix your design using an iron, following the instructions on the fabric paint.

Blow-painted skirt

Add a punky vibe to your skirt with bubbly blow painting.

1 Place a newspaper inside your skirt.

2 Place a straw in the paint and suck a little up your straw. Be careful not to get any in your mouth. Place your finger over the end of your straw and then remove to blow paint onto your skirt. Leave to dry. Ask an adult to fix your design following the instructions on the fabric paint.

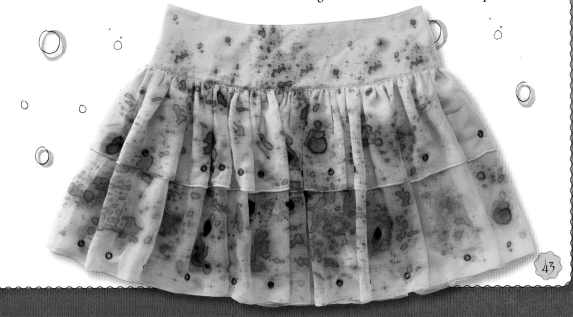

Sizzling sunglasses

Don't get left in the shade with these fabulous tropical glasses!

You will need

Add more jewels for an even more glamourous look

Tropical twist glasses

1 Trace and cut out the templates on page 63. Draw around them onto green and pink craft foam. Cut the circles in half and stick the smaller semi-circles onto the larger ones with craft glue.

2 Glue your watermelon wedges onto the corners of your glasses. Use a cocktail stick to dab glue onto some beads and stick them onto your wedges for the pips.

Palm beach glasses

1 Trace and cut out the palm tree template on page 63. Draw around your tree template onto green foam and the trunk onto brown foam, twice.

2 Cut the palms' trunks into sections and use double-sided sticky tape to attach them to the trees.

3 Glue your palm trees onto your glasses with some gems for coconuts. Glue some more gems to the frames for some extra bling.

Flirty frills

Get gorgeous by adding fabulous frills to your fashions!

You will need

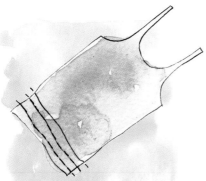

1 Cut three strips from the bottom of your vest, as shown. Don't worry if they aren't the same width, as this will add to the 'look' of the vest.

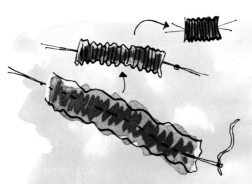

2 Sew a running stitch from one end of a strip all the way to the other end. Pull the thread so that the fabric gathers together into ruffles. Knot the ends. Do this for each strip.

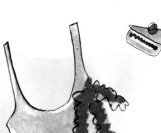

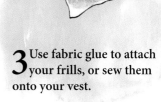

3 Use fabric glue to attach your frills, or sew them onto your vest.

Handy tip!

See page 62 for how to do running stitch.

4 Use a cocktail stick to dab glue onto some pearls and sequins and add them to your frilly vest design.

Fringe benefits

It don't mean a thing if you ain't got that fringe!

You will need

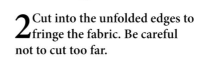

1 Measure and cut two pieces of scrap fabric measuring 20 x 7 cm. Fold both pieces in half.

2 Cut into the unfolded edges to fringe the fabric. Be careful not to cut too far.

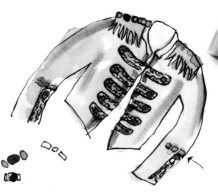

3 Use fabric glue to attach your fringing to the shoulders of your jacket. Leave to dry.

4 Glue some gems from a broken necklace, or bracelet to the top of the fringing and onto the cuffs. Leave to dry.

If you don't have gems, you could try gluing buttons, beads or sequins on instead.

Cowgirl wallet

Give your money some yeehaw with this super-cute cowgirl wallet!

You will need

2 Cut a 15 x 3 cm piece of brown felt and glue it to the inside edge of the 5 cm section so that it peeps out a little at the end. Use a pair of scissors to add some funky fringing. This will be the closing flap of your purse.

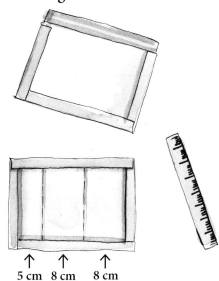

↑   ↑   ↑
5 cm   8 cm   8 cm

1 Measure and cut a 19 x 25 cm piece of denim. Fold over each edge by 2 cm and ask an adult to iron them down. Secure the hem with fabric glue. Measure and fold the denim into three and crease with an iron as shown.

Handy tip!
Always ask an adult for help when using an iron.

3 Measure and cut an 5 x 15 cm piece of patterned fabric and glue it to the outside of your purse above the fringing. Cut the tops of some paper fasteners and glue these to the front for a studded effect.

4 Fold the other short edge in and glue down the edges to make a pouch. Stick some self-adhesive Velcro dots to the top of the inside of the purse and to the inside flap so you can open and close it.

Experiment with different patterned fabrics!

Bright beanies

These snuggly beanies will keep your ears warm and you looking cool.

You will need

1 Place a small plate onto your jumper. Draw around the top of your plate to make the curved top to your hat. Remove the plate and extend the ends of your line the bottom of your jumper. Draw a border 2 cm above your hat shape.

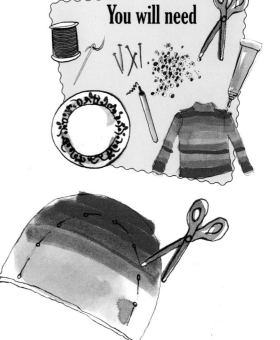

2 Stick pins around the first curved line you drew, pinning both layers of fabric together. Then cut along your border line. Save the rest of the jumper for your scraps box.

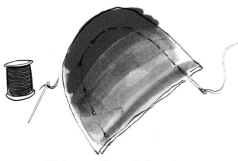

3 With a needle and thread, sew a running stitch around the line of pins, taking them out as you go. See page 62 for how to do a running stitch.

4 Turn your beanie right side out. Cut a little flower from your leftover jumper, and use fabric glue to attach it to the front of your hat. Glue some gorgeous beads to the centre. Sweet!

Why not make beanies to match all of your favourite winter outfits?

Glue on beads or pompoms to make your look unique.

Love hearts

Don't just wear your heart on your sleeve wear it on your vest and pumps!

You will need

I heart vest

1 Put a sheet of newspaper inside your vest. Starting at one shoulder, draw hearts all the way down and across your vest using a fabric-paint pen.

2 Leave to dry. Ask an adult to fix your design following the instructions on the pen.

I heart shoes
Give an old pair of shoes a new look by painting on some red hearts with acrylic paint. Sweet!

Why not shower all of your old clothes some love and sprinkle them with heart motifs?

Felt florals

Feel the flower power with bold felt blooms.

You will need

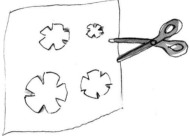

1 Trace and cut out the flower templates on page 63.

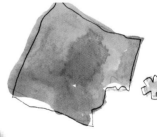

2 Draw around your templates onto some felt and cut them out. Use fabric glue to stick the smaller flower to the centre of the larger one.

3 Carefully wind a piece of sequin trim into a circle to make the middle of the flower. Dab glue onto the back using a cocktail stick and fix it to the middle of the flower. Leave to dry.

4 Glue or stitch your flower to your T-shirt.

Pretty lady

Trace a lovely lady onto your
Tee to transform it into
something fabulous.

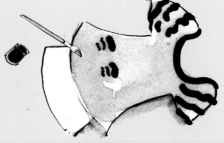

1 Draw a pretty face onto a piece of
white paper with a black marker pen.

2 Take a thin T-shirt and place your
design inside so that you can see it
through the fabric. Use it as a guide to
trace your design with black fabric paint.

3 Use blue, brown or green fabric paint
for the eyes, and pink for the lips.
Leave to dry.

4 Use more pink fabric paint to paint on
some hearts. Turn the T-shirt inside
out and ask an adult to fix your design
using an iron, following the instructions
on the fabric paint.

Hip hair bands

Don't feel tied down by dull hair ties, display your hairstyle with pride!

You will need

Multi-band magic

1 Place all four hair bands together. Wrap a bound feather around them.

2 Tie them together with a pretty ribbon. Cut the ends of the ribbon at a slant so that they don't fray. Glue the bow into place to make it extra secure.

Handy tip!
If you can't find bound feathers, simply wrap a coloured pipe cleaner around a craft feather for a similar look.

Rosette gorgeous

1 Cut a long strip of cotton jersey fabric. Starting at one end of your strip, use a needle and thread to sew a running stitch all the way up the middle. See page 62 for sewing tips.

2 Pull the threads at each end of the strip so the fabric ruffles together and makes a rosette shape. Knot the ends of your threads and use fabric glue to secure your rosette.

3 Glue your rosette ruffle to the hair band. Leave to dry.

Handy tips

Follow these utterly gorgeous tips for a truly, high-fashion finish.

Running stitch

Make a knot at one end of your thread, and then push your threaded needle in and out of the fabric you want to sew together. When you're finished, secure your stitches by sewing lots of stitches on top of one another.

In a fray?

Apply clear nail varnish to the edge of fabric to stop it fraying!

Inspiration kit

Save all your scrap pieces of fabric, old jewellery, and belts to cut up and re-use!

Hemmed in

Instead of gluing edges or hems, use iron-on fabric adhesive. Place a strip of adhesive inside the folded edge you want to hem. Put a damp cloth over the hem and iron over it. Always ask an adult to help you when using an iron.

Handy templates

Page 56-57

Page 8-9

Page 44

Page 8-9

Page 42

Page 8-9

Page 40-41

Page 20-21

Page 26-27

Page 45